An adult coloring book with ornametal elements in different animals that help you relieve stress and relax while coloring.

This side of the page will be intentionally filled
with black color in order to avoid color bleed through
while coloring.

You can have twice the fun coloring since the drawings
are repeated twice in case you want to color again
by using different colors.

Enjoy coloring!

Lola Donez

www.loladonez.com

Visit our website for freebies and subscribe to our newsletter to get notified when we release a new coloring book.

Made in the USA
Coppell, TX
08 December 2023

25629503R00046